Gates of Gold is about the discovery of gold, its legacy, and how it has defined and shaped Australia's identity.

READ about the discovery of gold in Australia and how it changed the face of Australia forever

DISCOVER how the golden frenzy brought about a population explosion with diverse communities and religions, different races, and different ideologies

LEARN about the arrival of the Chinese, who contributed greatly to the Australian story, but whose migration to the goldfields gave birth to racist, anti-Chinese sentiment.

FIND OUT why the discovery of gold had such a catastrophic impact on First Nations people and how they found ways to survive even when the odds were pitched so much against them

READ about a landscape transformed and the devastation of its ecosystems

and much more...

Gold! Hidden Stories of Australia's Past, Book 1

Gates of Gold

The Discovery of Gold, its Legacy and its Contribution to Australian Identity

Marji Hill

Published by The Prison Tree Press 2022

Copyright © 2022 Marji Hill

Copyright © 2022 Artwork and paintings by Marji Hill

Editor: Eddie Dowd

Image on cover: Pixabay

Paperback ISBN: 978-0-6454834-0-6
EBook ISBN: 978-0-6454834-1-3

 A catalogue record for this work is available from the National Library of Australia

The Prison Tree Press
Suite 124
1-10 Albert Avenue
Broadbeach, Queensland 4218
Australia

https://marjihill.com
https://www.fastselfpublishing.com

All rights reserved. No part of this book may be reproduced, stored in a retrieval system, or transmitted in any form or by any means, electronic, mechanical, photocopying, recording, scanning, or otherwise, without the prior written permission of the publisher.

Disclaimer
All the material contained in this book is provided for educational and informational purposes only. No responsibility can be taken for any results or outcomes resulting from the use of this material.

While every care has been taken to trace and acknowledge copyright the publishers tender their apologies for any accidental infringement where copyright has proved untraceable.

Every attempt has been made to provide information that is both accurate and effective, however, the author does not assume any responsibility for the accuracy or use/misuse of this information.

THE SERIES
Gold! Hidden Stories of Australia's Past

Book 1
Gates of Gold:
The Discovery of Gold, its Legacy and its Contribution to Australian Identity

Book 2
Shadows of Gold:
Eureka and the Birth of Australian Democracy

Book 3
Gold and the Chinese:
Racism, Riots and Protest on the Australian Goldfields

Book 4
Ghosts of Gold:
The Life and Times of Jupiter Mosman

Book 5
Blood Gold:
Native Police, Bushrangers & Lawlessness on the Australian Goldfields

Dedication

To My Grandmothers
who were part of Australia's gold rush

Margaret Hill (nee Shearer)
Lucy Matilda Hauenschild (nee Shaw)

Table of Contents

Chapter 1 — The Lure of Gold	1
Chapter 2 — Gold Rushes in Australia	17
Chapter 3 — The Oppression	31
Chapter 4 — Impact on the First Nations	41
Chapter 5 — The Golden Frenzy	55
Chapter 6 — The Chinese	69
Chapter 7 — Rape of the Soil	79
Sources	95
Questions For Further Consideration	99
About Marji Hill	101
Selected Books by Marji Hill	107

Acknowledgements

I acknowledge the Traditional Custodians of Country throughout Australia and their connections to land, sea, and community. I pay my respects to elders, past, present, and emerging and extend my respects to all First Nation peoples today.

In the spirit of reconciliation, my mission is to increase understanding between the First Nations and other Australians and to provide people from all over the globe some basic understanding of Australia's first people, their history, and cultures.

In my life I've been fortunate to have had several mentors. Alex Barlow, my late partner, would always say to me "If you manage your time well, you can achieve everything you want in life." That started my quest into the world of time management and learning how to maximise my productivity.

John Foley, barrister, helped me to expand my vision and has inspired me to make possible what seemed impossible. Sherien Foley has always been there to challenge and kickstart me and I remember her words when I hit rock bottom with my work many years ago and she said to me "There's only one way to go and that's up!"

This current series of books about gold grew out of a brainstorming session I had with my old friend, Gail Parr, while staying with her and her husband, George Sansbury at Maryborough in Queensland. We thrashed out the concept and from this grew these five books.

I would also like to acknowledge the late and great Jim Lynch who introduced me to the Charters Towers gold story many years ago and to his, son, Mark Lynch, Chairperson of the Citigold Corporation, who has always supported and encouraged my creativity in relation to the gold story both in books and in art.

And finally, thank you Eddie Dowd, my backstop and mentor, who has helped me get my books into their final form and ready for publication.

Marji Hill

"The irresistible attraction of gold in the nineteenth century brought to Australia thousands of gold-seeking travellers from around the world".

Marji Hill

Chapter 1 — The Lure of Gold

Migration to the goldfields

The irresistible attraction of gold in the nineteenth century brought to Australia thousands of gold-seeking travellers from around the world, lured by the discovery of gold in Victoria.

These were people seeking a new life of hope and prosperity who journeyed to down under by ship.

The cheapest way to make the journey from the British Isles and Europe was on a slow sailing ship. The trip would sometimes take as much as seven or eight months to reach its destination.

Life on board the ship was difficult. Rough seas, sickness, and poor quality food took its toll.

Some of the travellers wanting to prospect for gold died on the ships. Those that did make it to Australia were often weak and unfit for the hard work of mining for gold and the tough day-to-day life on the goldfields.

South Africa

My father's parents, Alexander Hill and his wife Margaret Shearer, together with Alexander's brothers, left Northern Ireland in the 1880s. They headed to Johannesburg in South Africa.

Like many other Irish men and women, they left their country to find a new life in another part of the world. They wanted to escape the hardships and tough living conditions so they migrated to other countries where they could get a fresh start with new opportunities.

The discovery of gold in South Africa offered opportunity. My family joined thousands of others searching for a new and better life.

The Johannesburg goldfield was proclaimed in 1886, the same year the Croydon goldfield in North Queensland, Australia, was proclaimed.

Within a year of the discovery of gold in Johannesburg, the whole Reef was estimated to have some 7,000 people, with 3,000 residing in Johannesburg itself.

The world's largest gold rush in history had begun and South Africa would never be the same.

The dream and prospect of a better life and fabulous wealth was obviously irresistible. News quickly spread around the world about what was happening.

My grandparents departed Ireland and became part of that mass of humanity heading for Johannesburg which they now saw as the land of opportunity.

My father's older sister, Christian Alice Hill, was born in Johannesburg around 1890. Between her birth and that of my father in 1898, the Hill family left South Africa and migrated to the goldfields in Western Australia. My father, Leslie Clement Hill, was born in a miner's tent at Coolgardie.

Coolgardie

Gold was discovered in Coolgardie in 1892 by Arthur Bayley and William Ford. They found more than 500 ounces of gold. A couple of weeks later, Bayley registered his claim in Southern Cross, 187 kilometres away.

Coolgardie is 550 kilometres east of Perth, Western Australia, and approximately 40 kilometres west of Kalgoorlie.

Irish prospector, Paddy Hannan, discovered gold on the Golden Mile a year later. This new gold district was 40 kilometres east of Coolgardie and was said to be the richest square mile of gold reserves in the world.

News spread like wildfire and triggered the last of the great Australian gold rushes.

During the 1890s on the east coast of Australia, people were suffering a severe depression.

Many migrated to the goldfields in the West, flocking to the blossoming gold rush towns in search of a better life.

Gold prospectors from all over the globe also arrived in Western Australia searching for a new life, wealth and prosperity.

After their long and difficult travels by ship they then had to face challenging journeys ahead of them to reach their destinations on the goldfields.

Woman in a miner's tent

Some found gold and others found only hardship — the housing was poor, there was a lack of fresh water and food, and a lot of sickness and death soon followed.

But the discovery of gold carved the way for an industry that has significantly contributed to the growth and development of the Western Australian economy. Within ten years the population almost quadrupled.

Overlanding

Earlier, in the 1850s, thousands of people from all over came to the goldfields in Victoria. This created a population explosion and the face of Australia changed forever.

Not only did people come from other parts of the world but also from within the Australian colonies itself. Men and women downed their tools and left their jobs with the goldfields their destination.

My maternal grandmother's parents, Henry and Henrietta Shaw, were among those who travelled overland to reach the goldfields. When they arrived at Wentworth at the junction of the Murray and Darling Rivers, Henry Shaw gathered his heavy equipment together and prepared for the long trek northwards. His rig consisted of a large wagon with horses and bullocks, and he was planning to do contract work along the way.

Bullock teams were a mainstay part of Australian life. Henry Shaw organised a covered wagon for the womenfolk - Henry's wife Henrietta, Henry's young sister Emily, and his baby daughter —my grandmother — Lucy Matilda Shaw, born in 1878.

After her birth, my ancestors loaded their bullock team with their possessions and set out from Melbourne on their expedition north. They travelled overland for nine years (1878-1887) on rough and often trackless country. They slowly continued north and eventually reached the goldfields of Croydon in Queensland's gulf country.

A year later in 1879 Lucy's brother, my great uncle Thomas Henry Shaw, was born at Wilcannia in New South Wales. After this the family continued north via Cunnamulla and Charleville in Queensland.

After arriving in Windorah, Henry Shaw decided to base himself at Canterbury a small town 80 kilometres west of there on the track to Birdsville.

Henry ran his carrier business together with a "Sly Grog" shanty. Another child, Florence, was born.

Tragedy also struck.

Emily, Henry's seventeen year old sister, suddenly died in 1882.

Croydon

After this, Henry decided to move on. The next stop was Connemara where he and his business partner purchased property. They experienced a couple of very dry seasons so they sold up. Henry and his family headed north to the Croydon goldfields in 1887.

Croydon was the last of the big goldfields in Queensland and was declared a payable field in 1886.

Henry, now 46 years old, decided to settle in Croydon and he developed his contracting business on the goldfields. The last of his two children were born at Croydon.

When the Croydon goldfields reached their peak in 1891 the gold mines had produced 72,000 ounces, had crushing mills with over 200 stamping heads, a population in excess of 6000 people and 58 hotels.

In this period gold yields from the Croydon goldfield were second only to those recorded at Charters Towers in North Queensland.

Mystique of gold

Such was the lure of gold that men and women uprooted their families, left their home countries of Ireland, Scotland, Wales, England, Europe and other parts of the world, and took perilous journeys to the continent down under.

Once they reached their destination the gold seekers took long hazardous treks across remote country in search of gold.

Gold has captured the minds of men and women throughout the ages. It's always had a magnetism, a mystique, seducing and intoxicating people, luring the unsuspecting into its spell.

More, gold has possessed people and haunted the minds of men and women since forever.

In Bernstein's words[1] gold has

motivated entire societies, torn economies to shreds, determined the fate of kings and emperors, inspired the most beautiful works of art, provoked horrible acts by one people against another, and driven men to endure intense hardship in the hope of finding instant wealth and annihilating uncertainty.

The metal gold

Time out for some interesting facts:

- The word "*gold*" comes from the Old English word for yellow which is "gelo";
- Gold is a metal that is prized because it is a metallic substance, estimated at comprising only 0.0000005 percent of the Earth's crust;
- Its chemical symbol is Au which is short for *aurum*. In Latin this means glowing dawn;

---

[1] Bernstein, Peter (2000) *The Power of Gold: the History of an Obsession.* New York, Wiley, p.1

- Gold, unlike other metals, is the only metal that is the colour yellow;
- As well as being prized for its beauty gold is malleable;

Gold is versatile with multiple uses. Some of its characteristics are:

- its use in electronics, ornaments and jewellery and advanced technology;
- can be beaten flat into sheets or leaves and an ounce of gold can even be stretched over a long distance;
- can be drawn into wire, cast, carved, and polished;
- can be embossed, hammered, cast, stretched and twisted;
- has a consistency that is nice to feel;
- can be made into thread and used in embroidery;
- doesn't tarnish;
- conducts heat and electricity, reflects light and is untouched by most acids;
- has the ability to melt at an amazing 1064 degrees centigrade and to boil at 2808 degrees centigrade.

GOLD "au"

Characteristics:
- Great beauty & nice feel
- Malleable & doesn't tarnish
- Conducts heat & electricity
- Reflects light & is untouched by most acids

Can be:
- beaten flat into sheets
- embossed, hammered, cat, stretched and twisted
- made into thread and used in embroidery
- melt at an amazing 1064 degrees centigrade, boil at 2808 degrees

Multiple uses: electronics, ornaments, jewellery, technology

Gold as investment

Throughout the centuries gold has been a symbol of wealth and power, a valuable commodity and a popular form of investment. Particularly in times of political turmoil and uncertainty, the tendency is for investors to put significant amounts of their money into gold. This is a method for safeguarding other capital investments.

It's a way of diversifying risk in an investment portfolio so it's really like insurance in times when the financial world is volatile.

Evidence of this happened on 8 March 2022 when the gold price went beyond US$2,000 an ounce because of world uncertainty surrounding the Russian aggression in the Ukraine.

The world's main trading currency is the United States dollar and when the dollar is fluctuating in value, gold is often used as a hedge.

It's an effective way of protecting capital against a weakening dollar. When the dollar falls gold tends to rise in value and when the dollar rises the gold price drops.

The legacy of gold

Gold in Australia is etched into the Australian psyche. It's been the catalyst for creators - in art, literature, music, and jewellery. It has formed part of legends associated with a bygone era.

Gold is pivotal in our national story. Gold features in defining moments of Australian history, and its discovery is engraved into the Australian story and its destiny.

One outcome of the discovery of gold was the population explosion which impacted the life and cultures of First Nations people. For example, the immigration that occurred formed

the basis of today's multicultural melting pot that now defines Australia. The Eureka Stockade on the goldfields at Ballarat in 1854 was a fight for the establishment of democratic rights that cemented the nature and direction of relationships between citizens and governments.

The many Chinese who migrated to the goldfields in search of greater prosperity stimulated the rise of anti-Chinese sentiment resulting in racial riots and prejudicial attitudes that still exist in our society to this day. Ongoing tension and resentment from the European gold miners towards the Chinese came to a head in anti-Chinese riots at Lambing Flat and other places.

Tensions between law and order created a legendary past of bushrangers. They were criminals who bailed up travellers, stole their money, gold, and possessions but were celebrated for their bravery, chivalry and their stance against corrupt colonial authorities.

In summary, while the outcome of the gold discoveries was progress and saw the creation of cities, transportation systems and generated great prosperity, it also had its negative side.

Its impact on the cultures of Australia's first people has been catastrophic — on the part of the colonial authorities and settlers, there was a fierce attempt to obliterate the cultural and spiritual life of Australian's First Nations people.

"Chiselled into the Australian psyche
was the dream of gold."

Marji Hill

Chapter 2 — Gold Rushes in Australia

Within a few months after the First Fleet sailed into Sydney in 1788 there was a convict called Daley. He claimed that he had discovered some gold.

In his efforts to prove that he had discovered it, Daley produced a lump of soil containing gold particles. This resulted in a rush to the area that Daley had identified.

But that was the end of the gold. Daley eventually made a confession and was severely punished. He had filed down a gold coin and salted the patch of earth in the hope of getting a pardon for making the discovery.

Daley was lashed mercilessly and was made to wear a canvas coat marked with the letter 'R 'for rogue[2]. A few months later he was hanged.

---

[2] Grassby, Al & Hill, Marji *Six Australian Battlefields:the Black Resistance to Invasion and the White Struggle Against Colonial Oppression.* North Ryde, NSW, Angus & Robertson, 1988, p. 205.

Californian Gold Rush

The Californian gold rush took place in the United States from 1848 to 1855.

As early as 1820 there were rumours of gold.

Some years later, James Marshall found alluvial gold there and gold fever hit.

Even in Australia at this time Sydney was gripped by gold fever.

In January 1849 six ships crowded with people lured by gold sailed from Australia for San Francisco. By the end of that year, many from Australia had joined the Californian gold rush.

Those from Australia seeking their fortune were called the "Sydney ducks" because they banded together in places like San Francisco, Sacramento and other centres.

During the Californian gold rush around 8,000 people from Australia had sailed across the Pacific to the United States to seek wealth and prosperity.

Many returned to Australia disillusioned.

Gold finds in New South Wales

Back in Australia in New South Wales, just after there were rumours of gold in California, Assistant Surveyor James McBrien in 1823 had found particles of gold near the Fish River not far from Bathurst in New South Wales.

Wiradjuri country

At this time British landholders had an insatiable greed for land. They had started to occupy thousands of hectares of Wiradjuri country along the Fish and Macquarie Rivers.

Tensions were developing between the Wiradjuri and the British as the red coated soldiers arrived with convicts.

The newcomers took over the best land and the permanent water supplies at gun point. This action forced the Wiradjuri from their traditional lands and denied them access to their food and water resources.

Bathurst became a military and supply base for the British aggressors.

The Wiradjuri witnessed the deadly danger of British firearms. They saw soldiers, chain gangs, and great herds of cattle and sheep moving into the places they traditionally occupied.

By 1820 the Wiradjuri were facing a very powerful, British presence in their country. They did not know it but the odds were being increasingly stacked against them.

The Wiradjuri were ready to fight as already blood had been spilt on their soil in defence of their land and families. Fighting west of the Blue Mountains had broken out as the British challenged the Wiradjuri nation.

The British not only wanted land but it looked as though the area was a rich and natural resource for gold.

More gold finds

Some sixteen years down the track in 1839, Count Paul Edmund de Strzelecki (1797-1873), the Polish explorer geologist and mineralogist, found traces of gold at Hartley in New South Wales.

However, Governor Sir George Gipps (1791–1847) requested that nothing be said.

Despite Strzelecki being keen to pursue his finds Governor Gipps was more concerned that a gold rush could sweep him and his rule into oblivion.

In 1844 when geologist and clergyman W. B. Clarke reported to Gipps and presented him with a gold sample he found at the Cox's River in the Bathurst district, once again the information was suppressed.

There were various other gold finds in New South Wales and Victoria but the discovery of gold did not become official until 1851.

In 1848 William Tipple Smith found gold near Bathurst. While Smith discovered gold his find was disregarded and the recognition went to Edward Hargraves.

Edward Hargraves

Edward Hammond Hargraves (1816-1891) is credited with finding the first payable goldfields at Ophir, near Bathurst, New South Wales.

Hargraves had been a sailor, a station overseer, a shipping agent and a publican before he went to California in 1849. However, he returned to New South Wales empty handed. He planned to win the reward being offered by the New South Wales government for the first find of payable gold.

He compared the gold-bearing geological formation he had seen in California with similar formations in Australia and decided they too must carry gold. Early in February together with his guide, John Lister, Hargraves rode out on horseback to Lewis Ponds Creek, a tributary of the Macquarie River near Bathurst.

After using his pick and shovel he filled and washed several pans some of which contained specks of gold. While he found a few specks in the creek he found nothing more.

Four men whom he had taught to pan, however, made a real find. Hargraves reported it to the authorities in Sydney and, sure of the reward, leaked the news to the press.

Within a few days 100 diggers arrived to make their instant fortunes.

By May the gold rush to Ophir had begun. By the end of May 1851 everyone in New South Wales knew about the Hargraves discovery. It was not long before a couple thousand people were mining for gold.

The gold rush was on!

Discovery of gold in Victoria

In the same year (1851), gold was discovered at Ballarat in the newly named colony of Victoria triggering the famous Victorian gold rush.

In the following year gold was found in larger quantities and these gold rushes of the 1850s were to change the nature and face of Australia forever.

In 1850 gold was found at Clunes. The following year (1851), James Esmond was credited with finding markable gold on Cresswick's Creek, a tributary of the Loddon River, even though evidence was forthcoming that First Nations people and settlers found gold before him.

Because gold seekers were flooding north to the newly discovered goldfields in New South Wales, the newly formed colony of Victoria offered an incentive to find gold there. The Victorian Government offered a reward of £200 to anyone finding gold within 200 miles of Melbourne.

Gold was found within months in Clunes, followed by discoveries at Ballarat, Castlemaine and Bendigo.

The historic gold rush at Ballarat occurred in August 1851. From this time to 1860 the Victorian goldfields which produced 25 million ounces of gold became the focus of attention in Australia.

It overshadowed the finds in New South Wales and the discoveries in Victoria went on to account for more than a third of the world's gold production in the 1850s.

Until the discovery of gold in north Queensland in the second half of the nineteenth century Victoria was Australia's most important gold producer.

Gold was discovered in Tasmania in 1852, in Queensland from 1857 and in the Northern Territory from 1871. In the last decade of the 1800s there were more gold rushes in Western Australia when gold discoveries happened at Coolgardie and Kalgoorlie[3].

Queensland gold

Queensland was the next State to be part of the Australian gold rush. It had already been found near Gladstone in 1857 and some years later in 1862 at Peak Downs.

As reefs of gold were discovered in Queensland, gold seekers arrived from all parts of Australia and New Zealand descending onto the goldfields.

Queensland had separated from New South Wales and became an independent colony in 1959. But at the time of the Queensland gold finds the colony was gripped by a crushing depression. The Bank of Queensland had closed,

---

[3] https://www.nma.gov.au/defining-moments/resources/gold-rushes

and there was discontent — there were open protests by those who couldn't get work.

But then James Nash discovered gold at Gympie near the Mary River in 1867. This perhaps saved the entire colony of Queensland from bankruptcy. The Queensland gold rush now gained momentum.

The Gympie find was followed by many other Queensland gold discoveries climaxing with the finds at Charters Towers in 1871, the Palmer River in 1873 and Croydon in 1886.

Western Australia

In the west of Australia across the continent, gold became publicly discovered in 1893 at Coolgardie. — it was first officially discovered at Coolgardie in 1892 by William Ford and Arthur Bailey.

The discoveries in the west triggered the last of the great Australian gold rushes.

During the 1890s in the east, Australia was gripped by a severe depression. Wanting to escape the unemployment, poverty and other ripple effects, gold seekers flocked to the goldfields in Western Australia searching for a better life.

In 1893 Irish prospector, Paddy Hannan together with Tom Flanagan and Daniel Shea discovered a goldfield said to be one of the richest in the world on the Golden Mile.

As the news about the new gold find spread, hundreds of diggers descended onto the field pegging out new claims at Kalgoorlie and then elsewhere in the region. Kalgoorlie became a mecca for thousands who had suffered the effects of the 1890s depression.

Companies were floated and the population swelled with people streaming in from the east.

After the initial gold discoveries many more were discovered north and south of the Kalgoorlie-Coolgardie region.

Finding new sites and developing gold mining in Western Australia brought prosperity to the west. The population there almost quadrupled within the space of a decade.

These discoveries carved the way for an industry that significantly contributed to the growth in the State with development reaching its peak between 1901 and 1905.

But gold mining in Western Australia was tough as the terrain was mostly desert. Water and food were in short supply. Diggers came unprepared; they suffered disease, dehydration, and heat stroke. Many died.

Despite these hardships, the allure of gold was all powerful and diggers continued to arrive in their thousands.

Australia prior to Federation

Australia's history and destiny was moulded in the years 1851 to 1901 by the discovery of gold.

Its population exploded going from approximately half a million to close on four million people.

While this golden era stimulated growth and prosperity and formed the basis for today's multicultural society, it was catastrophic for Australia's first people.

Not only that but the golden era gave birth to anti-Chinese sentiment that led to Australia's first race-based migration restrictions later fusing into the White Australia policy.

Miner's tool kit

"The double whammy or what can only be described as a tidal wave that hit Victoria in the 1850s with the discovery of gold saw not only the oppression of First Nations people but oppression of the miners who came to the goldfields to make their fortune. "

Marji Hill

Chapter 3 — The Oppression

When Captain James Cook on 19 April 1770 reached the east coast of Australia, his instructions from the British government were to take the eastern half of the continent for the British crown.

At Possession Island, off Cape York Peninsula in North Queensland, Cook took possession of the whole of the eastern coast in the name of King George III declaring that this newly found continent was *terra nullius*.

This meant that Australia was a land without people and that it was unoccupied and unowned. Therefore, the belief of the time was that the British could justify claiming the continent of Australia as their own[4].

---

[4] For more information about the "discovery" of Australia — Hill, Marji 2021 *First People Then And Now: Introducing Indigenous Australians.* 2nd ed. Broadbeach, Qld, The Prison Tree Press.

Ethnocentrism

Ethnocentrism means judging and evaluating other cultures according to the standards and customs of one's own culture. In simple terms it is thinking that one's own culture is superior to others.

For example, the English regarded their way of living and their values as being superior to that of all other cultures.

The English were ethnocentric.

They saw their own, their English culture, as the ideal and it was from this point of view that they judged all others. Social organisation and modes of social behaviour were evaluated on a scale relative to that of the English.

This English ethnocentrism evidenced itself in paternalism, superior attitudes, and derogatory statements about others.

Typical nineteenth century attitudes were based on evolutionary theory in its unilineal formulation[5].

---

[5] Hill, Marji & Barlow, Alex (1978) *Black Australia: An Annotated Bibliography and Teacher's Guide to Resources on Aborigines and Torres Strait Islanders*. Canberra, Australian Institute of Aboriginal Studies.

Darwin's theory of evolution, for instance, gave scientific support to the belief that Indigenous people of the world were inferior to the white race.

This nineteenth century mode of thinking was that Indigenous Australians would inevitably be displaced by the superior white race and that the First Nations people would be doomed to extinction.

Human development was seen as a straight upward climb from savagery to civilisation. European civilisation, with all its materialistic values, stood at the summit of this development and Indigenous people were seen as the bottom.

Given this attitude, First Nations people were seen as culturally and technologically inferior to the British and the Europeans - incapable of innovation, culturally static and defective in political and social organisation.

This kind of thinking was manifested in words like "primitive", "heathens", "savages", "a stone-age people", "pagans" and "Paleolithic survivals".

Colonisation of Australia

Captain James Cook's voyage of discovery to Australian shores in 1770 laid the foundations for the colonisation of Australia.

In North America settlements had been founded on land purchased from its native inhabitants. Cook, however, claimed territory along the east coast of Australia for Britain on the grounds that it was *terra nullius.*

This claim disregarded the First Nations and their relationship to their land.

Using this newly found continent as a convenient destination for its convicts, the British government brought prisoners, guards, soldiers, rebels and free settlers from many lands but especially England and Ireland to New South Wales.

Once they had served their time convicts became landholders. Settlers came to Australia and set up English institutions and forms of government that mirrored those of Great Britain, specifically based on occupation by military rule.

The British claimed the continent as theirs and they took over the traditional lands of the First Nations people using them for farming and setting up pastoral empires.

In addition, by the middle of the nineteenth century, it was discovered that parts of the Australian continent were rich in natural resources. With the discoveries of gold, the face of Australia was to undergo massive and rapid change.

Unlike Canada (and New Zealand), Australia had no treaties between its First Nations people and its colonial oppressors.

In 1835 John Batman did attempt to acquire land by treaty but the Governor at the time, Sir Richard Bourke declared that all such treaties were void as the British Crown, on the basis of Cook's proclamation, owned the entire continent.

The law of England

The law of England, including British property law, became the law of the Australian colonies on 26 January 1788. Without being informed or even consulted, First Nations people of Australia became subject to English law.

Following their defeat in the American Revolution in 1776, the arrival of the colonial forces from Britain on 26 January 1788 was the signal for the wars of resistance to begin.

British colonies were established beyond New South Wales and included establishments in Van Diemen's Land (Tasmania), Adelaide, Moreton Bay (Brisbane) and Port Phillip (Melbourne).

Rule by the British was reinforced by the military presence of British regiments. These Imperial regiments provided not only the occupation forces but also assisted the governors and administrators.

Early governors were like military dictators. The police were drawn from the military, the courts were military, and soldiers directed the building of roads, forts and public buildings.

Competition over land and resources quickly resulted in violence with historical records documenting numerous occasions when First Nations people were hunted down and brutally murdered.

The double whammy or what can only be described as a tidal wave that hit Victoria in the 1850s with the discovery of gold saw not only the oppression of First Nations people but oppression of the miners who came to the goldfields to make their fortune.

License-tax

In 1854 Ballarat was a city of tents. Trouble surfaced when the government imposed a mining tax.

This was not only a tax on what gold the miner was extracting but it was a license-tax for actually working a claim and for anyone working on the goldfields.

The miners protested and resisted but the government held its ground and continued to collect the tax, harshly and arbitrarily punishing defaulters.

The Eureka Stockade in 1854 was a battle inspired by political purpose. It was action against the constant harassment by police, the British regiments, and corrupt colonial administrators.

What happened at the Eureka was a victory for people's rights against the colonial oppressors. It was a fight for democracy. The miners took violent action against British colonial oppression to get rid of the licensing tax.

Not only was there over one hundred years of constant warfare as First Nations people resisted the takeover of their country there was the battle for democratic rights in the face of colonial oppression.

Gold! Hidden Stories of Australia's Past

Book 1

"The First Nations, their laws laid down in the Dreamtime, looked after their lands and ritually cared for their country with ceremony, songs, stories and art."

Marji Hill

Chapter 4 — Impact on the First Nations

What was acknowledged once as the unknown continent was in fact one of the earliest centres of civilisation in the world with its beginnings dating back 65,000 years if not more.

Prior to 1770 land that is now known as New South Wales, Victoria, Tasmania, Queensland and the rest of the continent was home to First Nations people.

Before the takeover of lands on the southern continent by the British, First Nations groups had defined territories. They knew the boundaries of their traditional lands, its physical features, its geography, the animals, birds, fish and plants.

The First Nations, their laws laid down in the Dreamtime, looked after their lands and ritually cared for their country with ceremony, songs, stories and art.

DREAMTIME

The ancestral beings travelled across the countryside in the Dreamtime shaping it, planting and peopling the land. Their journeys crisscrossed the Australian continent. Along these ancestral tracks are sites of special significance where certain events and incidents occurred.

All of these adventures happened in the Dreamtime - that time in the far distant past when all the land was flat, empty and dark.

When the creation adventures were over, they disappeared into the earth or sea or sky.

Following 1788 the British started to claim the traditional lands as theirs.

Pastoral empires were established and by the mid nineteenth century it was discovered that Australia was rich in gold.

First Nations people resisted this invasion. They fought to defend their country from the north to the south and from the east to the west.

Not one State in Australia was immune from resistance wars.

First Nations Australians of eastern Australia bore the full brunt of British occupation. It was they who were the first to experience the dispossession of their cultures.

What happened in New South Wales and Victoria was repeated throughout the continent in Tasmania, South Australia, West Australia, the Northern Territory and Queensland.

There was no discussion with the original people. There was no treaty, and tragedy continued to unfold.

Dispossession and near genocide characterised the occupation of the Australian continent for the next one hundred years. As white settlement spread throughout the country, para-military forces such as the Native Police were formed by the British to help combat the resistance.

Fighting moved over the Great Dividing Range with the crossing of the Blue Mountains in 1813. Following the example of the Eora in Sydney, their bravery unquestioned but with inadequate weapons to match the technological advantages of the invaders. The Wiradjuri challenged the British presence for many long and terrible months.

By the late 1830s the British had intruded into the lands of the Kamilaroi who were pushed from their water supplies and robbed of their game.

1838 saw the massacre of First Nations men, women and children at Myall Creek and by the end of the 1830s the resistance wars stretched from northern New South Wales to western Victoria.

Takeover of lands in Victoria

The takeover of First Nations lands in Victoria started in earnest in the 1830s.

In 1836 Major Thomas Mitchell, who was the then Surveyor General in New South Wales, set out from

Sydney to blaze the trail of British expansion further south.

The arrival of the British in Victoria irrevocably changed the lives of First Nations people. Initial conciliation gave way to European arrogance and First Nations resentment stemming from the settlers' idea of exclusive property ownership.

On 24 May 1836 when Mitchell's party was on the northern bank of the Murray River, it encountered a group of almost two hundred local inhabitants.

Mitchell decided to attack and ambushed the unsuspecting people. As they tried to escape the barrage by swimming across the river, they were shot in the water and those who reached the other side were also gunned down.

This was a massacre.

Mitchell crossed the Murray River into Victoria. He journeyed in a south-westerly direction and discovered the rich, fertile plains of western Victoria.

The arrival of pastoralists spelt gloom and doom for the Victorian First Nations people's traditional way of life. There was much resistance as the Victorians fought to defend "their" lands.

The seeds of war had been sown and it became clear that the British were grabbing all the country they could.

Initially, the First Nations Australians who fought to defend their country greatly underestimated the power and the long-range killing capability of European firearms. Encounters with the British were bloody.

The landscape of traditional lands underwent rapid change. As the British set up farms and pastoral properties with livestock and fences First Nations people could not access their hunting grounds.

They were hungry so they started stealing sheep, fruit and vegetables from the farms. The squatters retaliated by killing them.

The British pattern of invasion and destruction had been set. Within eighteen years (1836-1854) years of British incursion into the lands of what we now call Victoria there were at least 69 massacres of First Nation people [6].

Killing fields

The population in Victoria had grown to over half a million Europeans and Asians by 1861.

In those two decades from the 1830s to the 1850s the Koorie Heritage Trust Inc. documented in a map where First Nations people in Victoria were massacred [7].

These two decades can only be described as an era of killing.

First Nations Australians were massacred as they retaliated against the invasion of their lands by their British oppressors.

They had little chance against superior European weaponry - swords, muskets, pistols, shotguns, rifles, carbines and bayonets.

---

[6] Sovereign Hill https://sovereignhilledblog.com/2017/05/18/the-history-of-victoria/
[7] Culture Victoria "Massacre map" https://cv.vic.gov.au/stories/aboriginal-culture/indigenous-stories-about-war-and-invasion/massacre-map/

Dispossession

What happened to First Nations Australians in Victoria was catastrophic.

As the British claimed traditional lands for their own interests First Nations people experienced destruction of their own population, their culture and traditional country.

The discovery of gold on traditional lands added to this.

Despite these tragic events First Nations people displayed a resilience and a strength in the face of these troubling, dangerous and precarious times.

The First Nations people are credited with finding gold at Ballarat. In 1852 a prospector by the name of Paul Gootch wrote that a Wadawurrung man found a gold nugget while out searching for a horse [8].

Cahir [9] refers to Joseph Parker, the son of Assistant Protector of Aborigines Edward Parker, who claimed that:

---

[8] SBS "Gold" https://www.sbs.com.au/gold/rush-for-gold/
[9] Cahir, Fred https://press-files.anu.edu.au/downloads/press/p198511/pdf/ch022.pdf

"The first gold in the district [the Loddon valley] was discovered in 1849 by an Aboriginal boy in picking up what he supposed to be a stone to throw at a wounded parrot, but it turned out to be a nugget of gold!"

Again in 1871, gold was discovered by First Nations horse boy, Jupiter Mosman, at Charters Towers triggering the gold rush in North Queensland.

> Joseph Parker, the son of Assistant Protector of Aborigines Edward Parker, claimed that:
>
> "The first gold in the district [the Loddon valley] was discovered in 1849 by an Aboriginal boy in picking up what he supposed to be a stone to throw at a wounded parrot, but it turned out to be a nugget of gold!"

Law enforcement

Some Victorian First Nation people were recruited into a Native Police Corps and they became the first enforcers of the law on the goldfields.

Their duties were numerous. They conducted patrols and were on the lookout for bushrangers and prisoners. They policed frontier violence, assisted the gold commissioners, tracked people lost in the bush, provided escorts for travellers, and delivered mail.

The Native Police carried messages, they escorted gold to ensure that large amounts of gold reached its appropriate destination.

Sometimes Native Police had to go against their own people. If they didn't carry out the orders of their commandant they were threatened with punishment.

Role in local economy

Rather than simply becoming victims of the gold rush era, First Nations people were proactive in finding innovative ways to survive and stay on their country.

Cahir [10] makes mention of how in newspaper articles, letters, reminiscences and diaries there are references to First Nations people actively involved on the goldfields. They were entrepreneurial and eagerly participated in gold mining activities.

They were attracted to the goldfields. First Nations people were interested in the new wealth, new sights and sounds, and being able to form alliances with others caught up in the gold fever.

Sometimes First Nations people acted as guides to the miners, escorting them along traditional trading pathways. They helped miners to cross waterways and they assisted those who got lost in the bush. Given the First Nations skill of tracking they would help their European companions find their way and help them negotiate the local countryside.

First Nations people participated in the local economy. They would sell food and clothing to the

---

[10] Cahir, Fred (2012) Black Gold Aboriginal People on the Goldfields of Victoria, 1850-1870. Canberra: ANU Press, p.8.

miners. Some fossicked for gold themselves and would use nuggets for trade.

They sold possum skin cloaks which served as excellent clothing for warding off the cold. Even corroborees became popular events and were held to make money.

There were those First Nations people who organised their own successful gold mining parties across Victoria. Even members of the Native Police left the corps and went prospecting for gold.

Rather than just being casualties and victims of the British takeover of their traditional lands, First Nations people played a pivotal role on the goldfields and became operators in the local economy.

First Nations people demonstrated their resilience and their need to survive. They proved, as they did in the rest of Australia, that they were part of continuing, evolving cultures capable of change and adaptation.

"Australia was a whirlpool
sucking in those looking to make their fortune
in a golden frenzy."

Marji Hill

Chapter 5 — The Golden Frenzy

What happened as a result of the discovery of gold in Australia was in effect a tidal wave of people from all over the world who came to Australian shores to make their fortune.

Australia was a whirlpool sucking in those looking to make their fortune in a golden frenzy.

The discovery of gold, as it did in other parts of the world, offered people hope. It was hope and the prospect of prosperity that caused families to uproot from their countries and embark on life-changing adventures seeking lives for the better.

There was a population explosion after gold was found in 1851. Within twenty years the population grew from 430,000 to 1.7 million.

Those who migrated to the goldfields came from many parts of the world. There were the tin miners who came from Cornwell; there were those who came from other parts of Britain, Scotland, Ireland; there were the Chilean farmers and Africans;

soldiers came from Mexico; there were Germans, French, Italians, Americans, people from New Zealand, the Pacific, and the Chinese.

The common denominator was gold. They all wanted gold.

On the goldfields was a multitude of different ethnicities, different religions and different ideologies.

The gold discoveries of New South Wales and Victoria set in motion gold rushes in other parts of Australia.

The original plans may have been for these gold seekers to return rich to their homelands but the reality was the majority who came from the British Isles and Europe stayed in Australia.

Australia became a melting pot of all nations caught up in this frenzy for gold.

Women

The story of Australia's gold rushes is usually described in terms of being a domain for men. Gold mining is associated with men.

Among these gold migrants, however, were the women.

Women were active participants in the gold story. They accompanied their brothers, fathers and husbands to the goldfields. They were the wives, the mothers, the sisters, the girlfriends, and the children.

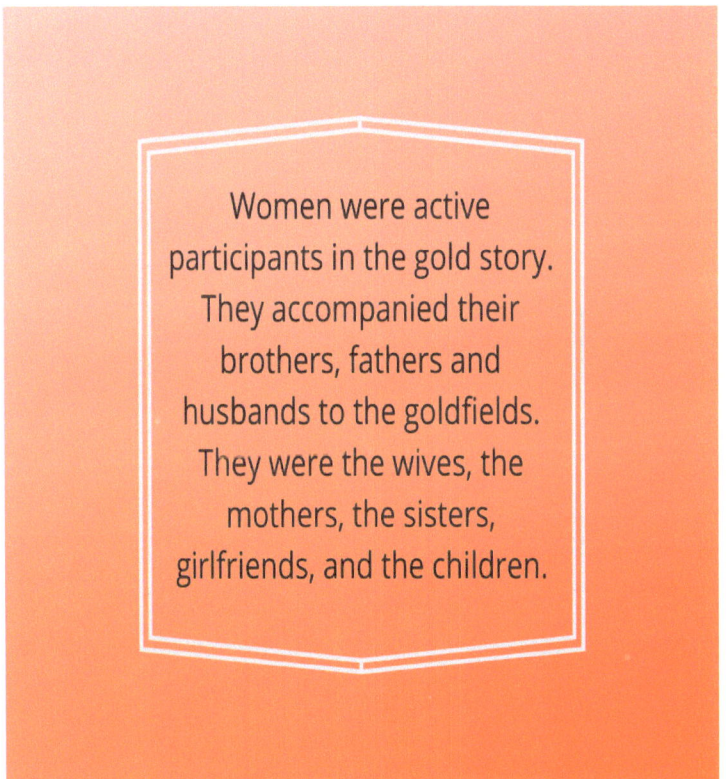

Women mined for gold themselves. It was in 1851 that a woman, Margaret Kennedy, who was one of the first to find gold in Bendigo.

There was an imbalance, though, in the ratio of women to men. After 1851 there were only 160,000 women to 600,000 men an imbalance that caused concern in a rapidly expanding population.

I reflect on the story of my own family. My father's mother - Margaret Shearer - as I said earlier came from Northern Ireland. After getting married to Alexander Hill she left Ireland and joined thousands of others looking for a fresh start, a new country, and a life that could offer hope and prosperity.

The dream and prospect of fabulous wealth was obviously irresistible. As news spread around the world about what was happening in South Africa, my grandparents joined the masses heading to Johannesburg to make their fortune.

After spending time on the goldfields in South Africa and giving birth to my auntie, Christian Alice, in Johannesburg, the Hill family left and headed for Australia.

The next bit of the jigsaw is that my grandmother gave birth in 1898 to my father, Leslie Clement Hill, in Coolgardie, Western Australia. The family story goes that he was born in a miner's tent on the goldfields.

Mining for gold was a unique way of life. Everyone faced their own challenges and problems. Those who made their fortunes often left the goldfields to retire, leaving behind those who hadn't yet had their lucky day.

Often, that day never came.

My grandmother was one of those women who followed her husband to the goldfields travelling across the world in the hope of making their fortune.

I can only use my imagination when I think about her. What were conditions like living in the golden era of South Africa? What were conditions like giving birth in a miner's tent in the West Australian goldfields at the end of the nineteenth century?

My grandmother would have faced domestic hardship as she and other women struggled to care for themselves and their children. They would have lived in tents or ramshackle huts.

This large, culturally diverse population from all over the world lived in cramped communities. Women's health must have been challenging and health care would have been sorely needed.

Domestic life was tough. Sanitation was poor. Infection was rife. There was little medical assistance.

Those who were nurses worked long hours often to the point of exhaustion. They experienced difficult conditions. Overcrowding was rife and you could imagine the extent of hygiene.

Typhoid was a constant threat. Sometimes the nurses got it and they too died.

Indeed, it was hazardous to have a baby so infant mortality was high.

Enterprising women

Women were forced to be enterprising on the goldfields.

In 1854 in Victoria, Wright [11] comments on the typical profile of a female migrant on the goldfields. She was between 20-34, newly married, and was raising a small family.

Life and times were precarious. Women, if they had lost their husbands to mining accidents or illness, had to bring in the money to support themselves and their families.

Housekeeping, cooking, laundering, child raising, child minding, and wet nursing were the activities that women mostly did.

Some were entrepreneurial. They might be company shareholders. A number were businesswomen running tearooms and boarding houses. Others established small shops selling groceries and baby clothes or other items that were needed on the goldfields.

There were the women who worked as domestic servants, dressmakers, milliners, barmaids and teachers. Some women sold alcohol or were

---

[11] Wright, Claire (2014) The Forgotten Rebels of Eureka. Melbourne, The Text Publishing.

prostitutes catering for the many single men on the goldfields.

Women's fashion of the day

Some women fossicked and panned for gold. They might work alongside their men who did most of the back breaking work but they would assist often washing gold dirt.

In the lead up to the Eureka Stockade in 1854, it was the women who worked through the night and produced the flag of the Southern Cross. It was made of silk with a blue background and a large silver cross.

In the battle itself there were women who got caught in the crossfire. A Mrs Catherine Smith died a few days later from her wounds and another woman is recorded as having been shot at Eureka.

Women mined for gold, they paid their taxes and fought for their rights.

The Jews

The influx of people to the Victorian goldfields seeking hope, a new life, and dreaming of great wealth came from all over the world. Amongst these were Jewish migrants.

The Jewish population grew after 1851 and by 1861 the Victorian Census recorded nearly 3000 Jews. They came from Britain, Germany, Poland and Eastern Europe.

Wright [12] mentions Rebecca Abraham who arrived in 1854 and married Polish-born, Alfred Isaacs. Their first son, Isaac Isaacs became Governor General of Australia in 1934.

> Sir Isaac Alfred Isaacs (1855-1948) was Governor-General of Australia, a High Court judge and a politician. His father, Alfred Isaacs was born in what was then Russian Poland. He left his country in the 1840s and settled in London. He married Rebecca Abrahams in 1849 and they migrated to Victoria in 1854 in the lead up to the Eureka Stockade.
> Sir Isaac Isaacs was a master lawyer and was one of the great judges of Australia's Federal history.

---

[12] Wright, Claire (2014) The Forgotten Rebels of Eureka. Melbourne, The Text Publishing.

Teddy Thonen, a German Jewish miner, was among those who were killed at the Eureka Stockade.

The Jews that joined the gold rush were business entrepreneurs rather than miners. Some did mine for gold but the majority became shopkeepers, hawkers, tradespeople, gold buyers, auctioneers, jewellers, silversmiths, tobacconists and publicans.

Jewish women took up occupations such as milliners, dressmakers and shopkeepers.

A significant percentage of business people in Ballarat were Jewish, and in contrast to the Chinese, they were more readily accepted into society. They contributed to the Ballarat community playing significant roles in politics and philanthropic organisations.

In 1853 the first *minyan* was said to have been convened in Ballarat for the Yom Kippur Kol Nidre (the Day of Atonement) service. Within two years, the Ballarat Synagogue had been formally incorporated and the Ballarat Hebrew Congregation met in Ballarat's *Clarendon Hotel*.

By 1861, the cornerstone was laid for the Ballarat Synagogue by Charles Dyte, a British-born businessman and auctioneer.

Dyte, who became the second president of the Ballarat synagogue, was active in supporting the miners' cause at the Eureka Stockade. Down the track he became the mayor of Ballarat.

Men and women originating from all parts of the world and all religions, some educated and some not, got caught up in the frenzy for gold.

"The high Asian presence on the goldfields was seen as a threat to the superior, ethnocentric attitudes of the British and Europeans and a threat, whether real or imagined, to the seat of power.

The outcome was race-based migration restrictions that fused into the White Australia policy."

Marji Hill

Chapter 6 — The Chinese

The largest non-European group of gold miners that were caught up in the golden frenzy were the Chinese.

By the mid-1850s, thousands of Chinese migrants descended onto the Victorian goldfields. In 1861 the goldfields in Victoria - Ararat, Ballarat, Bendigo, Castlemaine, and Maryborough - had around 24,000 Chinese. There were over 11,000 Chinese in many New South Wales towns like Armidale, Tamworth, Braidwood, Young, Tumut and Mudgee [13].

Christina Sexton, referring to the work of Dr Benjamin Mountford, said that in 1859 approximately one in five men on the goldfields

---

[13] National Museum of Australia
https://www.nma.gov.au/explore/features/harvest-of-endurance/scroll/chinese-gold-miners

were Chinese [14] — revealing how strong this Asian presence was in Australia.

While the English had seized the ruling power in the land of opportunity down under and laid down the laws of England, it was during the time of the gold rushes that the Asian presence made its mark on the country that was geographically Asian.

Chinese migration

Indonesian fishermen - the Macassans - visited the northern shores of Australia every year for several hundreds of years to collect trepang for the Chinese market.

Trepang was a highly prized delicacy in China so there was a trading connection for centuries between China and Australia long before the British arrived in 1788.

---

[14] Sexton, Christine "Turning points in history - the gold rush" https://www.impact.acu.edu.au/community/turning-points-in-history--the-gold-rush

Macassans

For a period of several hundred years to just after the conclusion of the nineteenth century Macassans from Indonesia visited northern Australia. They were fishermen and they fished for the sea slug called trepang, a prized delicacy in Chinese cuisine.

Each year they came and set up settlements on sheltered beaches along the coast of Arnhem Land. They set up processing plants for the trepang also known as beche-de-mer. Once treated and smoked it was taken back to Macassar to trade with the markets in Asia.

The Californian goldfields were known as Old Gold Mountain. Arriving in their thousands, the Chinese called the Australian goldfields New Gold Mountain, their population peaking around 40,000 in the early 1860s.

The vast majority of Chinese were men who mostly came from Guangdong, a province in China.

After a discriminatory tax by the colonial authorities was laid on ships carrying Chinese to Australia, ship captains dropped their passengers off in ports hundreds of kilometres away from their destination. Robe in South Australia became a popular drop off port. Around 17,000 Chinese walked four hundred kilometres to the goldfields.

Only a small minority of Chinese miners paid their own way to Australia. Most came on the credit-ticket system and were sponsored by merchants in Hong Kong and Australia.

Inevitably this high Asian presence was a threat to the superior, ethnocentric attitudes of the British and Europeans and a threat to the seat of power.

The outcome was race-based migration restrictions that fused onto the White Australia policy.

Chinese work ethic

The Chinese were successful with their gold mining gold efforts. Much of their success was attributed to being well organised. They worked their diggings in groups operating in groups of 30 to 100 men under the direction of a leader.

They were monitored by headmen or bosses in association with fraternal organisations such as secret societies. Most Chinese men were members of these organisations or the Hung Men brotherhood. This extensive social network ensured that they got employment, and had their needs catered for.

Chinese women folk remained in China to look after the old and the young. This meant that in Australia the Chinese population was male and was mostly single.

Only a small minority of men married and if they did it was usually to European or First Nations women.

Not only did the Chinese mine for gold they were entrepreneurial. They developed businesses - restaurants, Chinese medical clinics, opium dens, and market gardens - all businesses that served the needs of miners on the goldfields.

Anti-Chinese sentiment

Anti-Chinese sentiment grew. For a start they looked different; to the Europeans they looked peculiar.

They spoke a different language, they wore what appeared to be strange clothing, they had different food and different customs.

They would walk in long files to the goldfields wearing loose garments that looked like women's clothing, wearing long pigtails, and high conical hats.

The Europeans regarded the Chinese with suspicion.

The Chinese became known as "Celestials" and for the Anglo-establishment they became an increasing concern.

Chinese mining worker

In New South Wales a double miner's tax was imposed on people who included not only Chinese but all non-British subjects. Victoria went further and imposed ten pound poll tax on the Chinese when they arrived.

The population of Chinese miners dropped when the gold deposits began to dwindle in Victoria and New South Wales. However, there were more gold discoveries in the north.

This caused an influx of Chinese to the new goldfields in Queensland.

In far north Queensland in the 1870s there was a surge in population on the Palmer River goldfields. By 1877 over 90 per cent were Chinese[15], the Palmer River hosting around 20,000 from China.

After gold petered out many of the Chinese miners returned to their families in China but some, however, stayed in Australia.

---

[15] Kirkman, Noreen (1986) "Chinese Miners on the Palmer" https://espace.library.uq.edu.au/

"Country was turned upside down, it was upset, ecosystems were destroyed, and what were once pristine environments were no more."

Marji Hill

Chapter 7 — Rape of the Soil

From 1788 with the coming of the British to their newfound southern continent the landscape of Australia was changed forever.

As explorers ventured towards new horizons and graziers grabbed land to establish large pastoral holdings not only did they adversely affect the traditional ways of life for Australia's First Nation people but they transformed the landscape.

The intrusion of the British into south-eastern Australia saw land being taken over and divided up into individual "private" properties. The British took ownership of the property.

Country was changed by fences, cattle, sheep, horses, and buildings, and protected by guns. Australia's First Nations people lost their land. In addition, diseases were introduced and this together with settler violence, had a devastating impact on the lives of the original inhabitants later grouped and became known as Aborigines, not by their original names, e.g., the Wadawurrung people.

Epicentre of gold

Ballarat in 1851 became the epicentre of European settlement and gold mining in Australia.

The outcome for the local Wadawurrung people can only be described as near genocide.

Within the space of just seventy years around 90 per cent of Wadawurrung people were wiped out.

Wright [16] estimates the numbers — prior to 1788 there were up to 3240 members of the twenty-five Wadawurrung language groups; by 1861 only 255 First Nations people remained.

The devastation for First Nations people in Victoria was magnified with the arrival of a second tidal wave.

---

[16] Wright, Claire (2014) *The Forgotten Rebels of Eureka*. Melbourne, The Text Publishing

These were the thousands of people who migrated to the goldfields in the 1850s seeking their fortunes in gold.

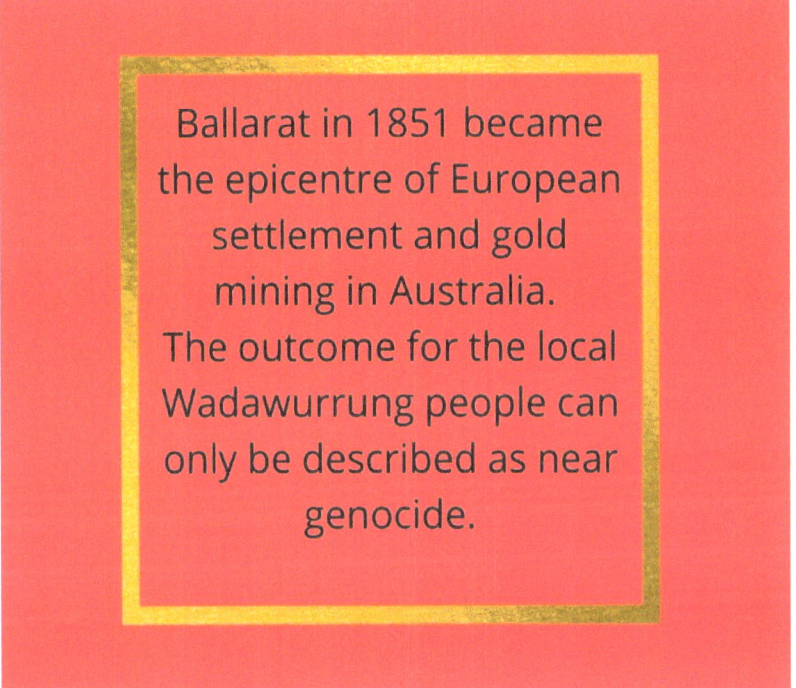

Ballarat in 1851 became the epicentre of European settlement and gold mining in Australia. The outcome for the local Wadawurrung people can only be described as near genocide.

The advent of the gold rush in Victoria disrupted and rapidly destroyed ecosystems. Enormous pressure was put on the native flora and fauna.

The discovery of gold might have been a sign of "progress" with its associated great energy, population growth, productivity, and the establishment of towns and infrastructures. It propelled the country's economy, stimulated industry, and grew its population.

But not everyone benefited from this new prosperity. As settlement spread, First Nations people were forced off their country.

While the gold rushes did equate with prosperity on the other side of the coin, the discovery of gold was incredibly destructive.

Destruction

Gold mining has been a destructive industry [17]. As in other parts of the world, it has displaced communities and it did this in Australia with the First Nations.

It contaminated drinking water, hurt workers, and destroyed pristine environments. It polluted water and land with mercury and cyanide endangering the health of people and ecosystems.

---

[17] Earthworks "Dirty gold's impact" https://earthworks.org/campaigns/no-dirty-gold/impacts/

The soil was upturned. Holes were dug. Structures were built and eventually buildings were erected.

There was a population explosion. People came with the expectation of making a fortune and with them came the tools of trade: axes: picks, shovels, gold pans.

Ecological impact

The country was turned upside down, it was upset, ecosystems were destroyed, and what were once pristine environments were no more. Many animals and plants became extinct. In Ballarat it is estimated that approximately one metre of topsoil had been removed by the diggers [18].

While sheep grazed, traditional grasslands were decimated. Sheep caused the near extinction of the Morning Daisy one of the staple plant foods of the local people [19].

---

[18] Sexton, Christine "Turning points in history - the gold rush" https://www.impact.acu.edu.au/community/turning-points-in-history---the-gold-rush

[19] Sovereign Hill https://sovereignhilledblog.com/2014/09/01/the-environmental-impact-of-the-gold-rush/

As diggers mined for gold polluted sludge was discharged directly into Victoria's rivers and streams. On the goldfields large stretches of forests were cut down.

The transformation of the country was abrupt. Horses, cattle and sheep scarred the landscape. Men and women scarred the landscape.

The newcomers, in effect, re-designed Country.

Gold diggers needed firewood. They needed wood to erect their buildings and shops; they needed wood for the boards that had to reinforce tunnels.

The countryside became pitted with holes.

The ecological impact of gold mining was severe.

Polluted waterways

Waterways were modified throughout gold mining regions and sometimes men had to divert or re-route whole creeks and rivers to access water in another area.

Where there was once clear and fresh water was now dirty and contaminated.

There was toxic mining waste. This contained dangerous chemicals like arsenic, lead, mercury, acids, cyanide and petroleum by-products.

This noxious waste would have contaminated the waterways. Not only was it toxic to aquatic life but also it meant drinking water was ruined.

The health of those on the goldfields was compromised. In addition, this toxic waste would work its way into the food chain causing sickness in people and in animals both in the immediate area as well as the cities that relied on farms for food.

Dangers

While some gold seekers struck it rich and made their fortune others were not so successful. For many there was no return on their investment of physical hard labour and deprivation.

The goldfields were hazardous places. If diggers consumed too much alcohol or if they were inexperienced with this kind of work they were in danger of suffering serious accidents or even death on the goldfields — drownings, cave-ins, accidents and violence were common.

There are reports of shocking mining accidents. There are stories of men getting buried alive; the murders, the treacherous roads, the risk of getting lost, assault, and robbery by bushrangers. There were plenty of mining deaths and others dying from unforeseeable circumstances.

It was common for men and women to carry pistols and tomahawks for protection.

Human interference on the goldfield environment was extreme not to mention the dust, the flies, the mud and the swamps.

Relics of gold mining days

Any tourist today who visits sites of the gold rush will come across ruins and relics of the bygone era. These relics are testimony to the rich gold mining days of Australia.

Throughout the gold mining regions there are abandoned mines and mineshafts that gave vertical access to an underground mine.

The landscape is literally littered with these relics of the past - old engine parts, gold puddlers, ore batteries, poppet heads, boilers. Museums stand testimony to the by-gone gold eras.

In Victoria at the Pink Cliffs Geological Reserve, a hydraulic sluicing site washed away the top layer of earth to reveal dramatic, colourful cliffs.

The Black Hill Reserve in Ballarat is an impressive patch of parkland with remnants of open cut and shaft mining.

Blue Waters is a beautiful waterhole located within the Creswick Regional Park and was once an open cut mine.

Etched into the landscape are images of past mining which produced a changed and modified environment.

Trees, soil, waterways, air - all were profoundly impacted by the population boom and the mining practices of these gold mining immigrants.

Today, these practices are universally seen to be environmental vandalism and are not tolerated in Australia, resulting in harsh penalties.

Looking Down a Mine Shaft

Gold mining today

Throughout time, since gold has been one of the world's most valuable of commodities, its darker side has been its harsh footprint on the environment.

Because there are so many ecological challenges associated with gold mining, gold mining corporations today have put in place a swathe of safeguards to mitigate against environmental damage.

One of the worst practices has been the use of cyanide in mining operations.

The aim of the Citigold Corporation at Charters Towers, for instance, is to extract gold from rock without cyanide or a tailings dam.

Scientists and researchers throughout the world have found ways to alleviate the environmental impact of the gold mining industry. Australian corporations involved in gold mining today work on practising and upholding high standards of occupational health, safety, and environmental standards.

Gold mining today – Down the decline at Charters Towers

An emerging national identity

The discovery of gold changed forever the face of Australia.

A kaleidoscopic collection of humanity populated what once was the unknown continent, the majority of faces on the goldfields being white. However, by the end of the 1850s one in five men were Chinese.

Chinese Australians have contributed greatly to the Australian story but their migration to the goldfields gave birth to anti-Chinese sentiment.

The hefty Asian presence was a threat to Anglo supremacy and the superior, ethnocentric attitudes of the British and the Europeans. It threatened the seat of power whether real or imagined and gave rise to growing racist, anti-Chinese feelings that manifested in riots in both New South Wales and Victoria.

The outcome was race-based migration restrictions that later were transformed into the White Australia policy.

Gold resulted in a population explosion with diverse communities representing different religions, different races and different ideologies. From this emerged a new, national identity - a land of plenty, wealthy, a liberal society with a standard of living that was the envy of the rest of the world [20].

---

[20] National Museum of Australia "Gold Rushes" https://www.nma.gov.au/defining-moments/resources/goldrushes#:~:text=In%201851%20gold%2Dseekers%20from,of%20a%20new%20national%20identity.

Great energy and massive productivity characterised this golden era. Along with it and creating the Australian story came the telegraph, steamships, railways, cities and towns - all the symbols of a boosted economy and progress.

In summary

Australia's huge gold reserves attracted men and women from many parts of the globe. With them came fresh political ideas and progressive thinking. This new ideology became a threat to the colonial establishment resulting in tensions and ultimately culminating in the Eureka Stockade.

The impact of the gold discoveries together with British confiscation of traditional lands of Australia's first people was catastrophic. It represented a fierce attempt by colonial authorities and settlers to obliterate the cultural and spiritual life of Australia's First Nations people.

As settlement spread, the original people were forced off their country, their natural resources and landscape devastated. Country was turned upside down.

Land was taken over by British intrusion, divided up into individual properties, and transformed by fences, cattle, sheep, horses and buildings, a land taken and controlled by Anglo supremacy.

After gold was discovered in 1851 the colonial authorities needed help in bringing law and order onto the goldfields and for this they got the assistance of paramilitary police and the military.

As desperate diggers flooded to the goldfields there was a huge increase in crime. Not only was there lawlessness but for travellers on routes between the diggings and the cities armed robberies and violence was common.

As the gold rushes brought thousands of gold seekers and wealth to the bush, gold became a target for theft. Bush ranging gained momentum and the bushranger became part of the Australian identity.

In history, often their crimes were forgotten, and they became remembered for their daring exploits, their ability to survive in the bush, their horsemanship and their challenge to the colonial authorities.

With Australia's huge gold reserves attracting people from many countries came fresh political ideologies and new ways of thinking. These new viewpoints were another threat to the colonial establishment.

And now…

In the next book in this series, *Shadows of Gold,* discover the seeds of rebellion and how these tensions ultimately culminated in the Eureka Stockade, a battle inspired by political purpose.

What happened at Eureka was a victory for people's rights against the colonial oppressors.

It was a fight for democracy.

Sources

The author would like to acknowledge the following sources of information:

Bernstein, Peter (2000) *The Power of Gold: the History of an Obsession*. New York, Wiley.

Cahir, Fred https://press-files.anu.edu.au/downloads/press/p198511/pdf/ch022.pdf

Cahir, Fred (2012) *Black Gold Aboriginal People on the Goldfields of Victoria, 1850-1870*. Canberra: ANU Press.

Culture Victoria "Massacre map" https://cv.vic.gov.au/stories/aboriginal-culture/indigenous-stories-about-war-and-invasion/massacre-map/

Earthworks "Dirty gold's impact" https://earthworks.org/campaigns/no-dirty-gold/impacts/

Grassby, Al & Hill, Marji (1988) *Six Australian Battlefields: the Black Resistance to Invasion and* the White Struggle Against Colonial Oppression. North Ryde, NSW, Angus & Robertson.

Hill, Marji (2021) *First People Then and Now: Introducing Indigenous Australians.* Broadbeach, Qld, The Prison Tree Press.

Hill, Marji & Barlow, Alex (1978) *Black Australia: An Annotated Bibliography and Teacher's Guide to Resources on Aborigines and Torres Strait Islanders.* Canberra, Australian Institute of Aboriginal Studies.

Kirkman, Noreen (1986) "Chinese Miners on the Palmer" https://espace.library.uq.edu.au/

National Museum of Australia "Gold Rushes" https://www.nma.gov.au/defining-moments/resources/gold-rushes#:~:text=In%201851%20gold%2Dseekers%20from,of%20a%20new%20national%20identity

National Museum of Australia https://www.nma.gov.au/explore/features/harvest-of-endurance/scroll/chinese-gold-miners

SBS "Gold" https://www.sbs.com.au/gold/rush-for-gold/

Sexton, Christine "Turning points in history - the gold rush" https://www.impact.acu.edu.au/community/turning-points-in-history---the-gold-rush

Sovereign Hill https://sovereignhilledblog.com/2014/09/01/the-environmental-impact-of-the-gold-rush/

Sovereign Hill https://sovereignhilledblog.com/2017/05/18/the-history-of-victoria/

Wright, Claire (2014) *The Forgotten Rebels of Eureka*. Melbourne, The Text Publishing.

Gold! Hidden Stories of Australia's Past

Book 1

Questions For Further Consideration

What was the significance of major historical events that shaped Australia's identity?

What are Australian gold mining corporations doing to rehabilitate the landscape?

What has been the highest price for gold each year over the past 10 years?

Gold! Hidden Stories of Australia's Past

Book 1

About Marji Hill

Artist & Author

Marji Hill, artist and painter since childhood, runs her art career alongside her career as an author.

Marji is a highly respected international author as well as a seasoned business executive, researcher, and coach.

She is passionate about promoting understanding between Australia's first people and other Australians.

Marji has fostered the spirit of reconciliation in all her writings since she was Research Fellow in Education at the Australian Institute of Aboriginal and Torres Strait Islander Studies (AIATSIS) in Canberra.

From 2008 to 2011, Marji was Deputy Chairperson of the Mosman Branch of Reconciliation Australia in Sydney.

Following her Education Research Fellowship at AIATSIS in 1976 Marji, together with her late partner, Alex Barlow, produced more than seventy (70) books on all aspects of the First Nations people including the critical, annotated bibliography *Black Australia*.

In 1989 Marji was the Project Coordinator and one of the researchers and writers of *Australian Aboriginal Culture* the official Australian Government publication on First Nations people.

In 1988 her work of non-fiction *Six Australian Battlefields*, which she co-authored with Al Grassby, was published by Angus and Robertson. A decade later it was re-published by Allen & Unwin as a paperback edition.

Her nine-volume encyclopaedia, *Macmillan Encyclopaedia of Australia's Aboriginal Peoples* was published in 2000 and in 2009 she published *The Apology: Saying Sorry To The Stolen Generations*.

Marji's more recent publications extend to self-improvement and self-help with books like *Staying Young Growing Old* and *Inspired by Country* a self-help book about painting with gouache.

Marji's artworks range from very large oil paintings on canvas (her largest being 213 x 167cm) to very small works on paper - gouache being a favourite medium.

Black/white relations, reconciliation, Eureka, and the discovery of gold are common themes not only in her writings but also in her art.

Her small paintings are simple responses to land and sea environments.

Painting has been a lifetime passion for Marji. She remembers as a child winning first prize for a painting she exhibited at the Southport agricultural show. Then in her teens for two years in a row she won the Sunday Mail Child Art Competition in Queensland with her winning paintings getting full coverage in colour in the newspaper.

Marji's formal art training took place in the 1980s at the Canberra School of Art which in 1992 became ANU School of Art & Design.

As soon as she completed her Master of Arts Degree in Anthropology at the Australian National University (ANU), Marji went on to get a Post Graduate Diploma in Painting. She has held eight solo exhibitions in Canberra, Melbourne and Sydney and she has participated in various group shows.

One of her large paintings was included in the 2004-2005 Art Gallery of Ballarat's Travelling Exhibition *Eureka Revisited: the Contest of Memories*. This exhibition travelled to Melbourne, Canberra and Ballarat - part of the 150-year celebration of the Eureka Stockade.

Two of her large paintings were commissioned by the Citigold Corporation. One was on display for many years in the foyer of Jupiter's Casino in Townsville until the casino was sold, becoming the The Ville Resort-Casino.

Jupiter's Lucky Strike celebrates the discovery of gold by First Nations boy, Jupiter Mosman in 1871 at Charters Towers in North Queensland. This painting today hangs in the offices of the Citigold Corporation in Charters Towers.

The other, a portrait of Jupiter Mosman resides in the World Theatre in Charters Towers.

Marji's paintings are in many private collections both in Australia and overseas and she is represented in the Art Gallery of Ballarat and Ballarat and Sydney campuses of the Australian Catholic University.

For many years Marji travelled extensively both within Australia and internationally, working as a consultant, doing speaking engagements, motivating people, and developing her art career.

Marji resides in Surfers Paradise. She pursues her interests of writing, painting, mentoring, publishing, and internet marketing.

If you would like more information about Marji, her work and her writing please visit

https://marjihill.com

Selected Books by Marji Hill

Self-improvement/Self-Help

Hill, Marji (2014) *Staying Young Growing Old.* Broadbeach, Qld, The Prison Tree Press.

Hill, Marji (2020) *How Big Is Your Why? An Author's Guide to Time Management and Productivity to Achieve Transformational Results.* Broadbeach, Qld, The Prison Tree Press.

Hill, Marji (2020) *A Create and Publish Toolbox: 101 Prompts In A Guided Journal To Help You Write, Self-publish, And Market Your Book On Amazon.* Broadbeach, Qld, The Prison Tree Press.

Hill, Marji (2021) *Inspired by Country: an Artist's Journey Back to Nature, Landscape Painting with Gouache.* Broadbeach, Qld, The Prison Tree Press.

First Nations

Hill, Marji (2021) *First People Then and Now: Introducing Indigenous Australians.* 2nd ed. Broadbeach, Qld, The Prison Tree Press.

Hill, Marji (2021) *Australian Aboriginal History: 5 Stories of Indigenous Heroes.* Broadbeach, Qld, The Prison Tree Press.

Gold

Hill, Marji (2022) *Shadows of Gold: Eureka and the Birth of Australian Democracy.* Broadbeach, Qld, The Prison Tree Press. (Gold! Hidden Stories of Australia's Past, Book 2)

Hill, Marji (2022) *Gold and the Chinese: Racism, Riots and Protest on the Australian Goldfields.* (Gold! Hidden Stories of Australia's Past, Book 3)

Hill, Marji (2022) *Ghosts of Gold: The Life and Times of Jupiter Mosman.* (Gold! Hidden Stories of Australia's Past, Book 4)

Hill, Marji (2022) *Blood Gold: Native Police, Bushrangers & Lawlessness on the Australian Goldfields.* (Gold! Hidden Stories of Australia's Past, Book 5)

www.ingramcontent.com/pod-product-compliance
Lightning Source LLC
Chambersburg PA
CBHW041459010526
44107CB00044B/1509